WHAT REALLY HAPPENS

HAPPENS

by

BRANDY **D**OLEN

ISBN: 1466242663
ISBN 13: 9781466242661

To Milburn Dolen
Carol Dolen
Kerry Riley
Meghan Dolen
Jake Dolen
Jordan Creel
Thank You For Being The Most Amazing
Family I Could Ever Ask For. Together, You
Have Been My Rock All Along.

To Dave Richardson
Doug Edwards
Valley And Rachel
Nettwerk Songs Publishing
Thank You For Supporting Me In This
Endeavor.
Because Of Your Help I Was Able To Give
Life To My Past.

To Hayley Curry
Thank You For Being There For Me
Throughout
The Years. You Taught Me How To Love
The Little Things In Life.
To The Woman Whom I'll Never Know And
Never Forget
Thank You, You Are
Truly My Angel.

This book is dedicated to all the lost voices
And the unheard cries.
I Promise There Is Hope.

What do you do when someone has taken away your will to live? When they make you feel unworthy of the air you breathe? What is truly the next step? How do you deal with a constant tormentor for three years straight?

I took steps to take my own life. I wrote death notes and left them by my bedside and hoped not to wake up in the morning. I became an insecure, suicidal wreck.

I wrote this story for a few reasons. I need the world to know what really happens to today's youth. Everyone recognizes bullying as a severe problem, but few know how to really deal with it. Many adults have written books about bullying, suicide, and all the signs to watch for it. Adults only receive bits and pieces of the truth. As someone who has been through a tortuous situation that led to multiple attempted suicides and medical problems I find it is my duty to try and prevent this from happening to others. I will walk you through my years of hiding, dealing, and coping with wanting to die every day of my life. I hope this book will change your life in a positive manner. If it changes or helps one person, I will feel satisfied knowing that I may have saved a life by failing to take mine.

Scene: Eleven-year-old girl, smart, well liked by most peers, and has a good family.

Inference: She has a good life with the occasional road bump along the way.

Truth: She is beginning life by thinking the only possible way to continue is by ending it.

Get ready for the truth about what really happens.

BACKGROUND

I used to love school. I had a passion for learning. I would have rather written an essay then play outside with friends. I poured my all into each and every assignment. I was definitely what one may call nerdy, but I was so much more than that. School was where I always wanted to be. It was what I was best at, my hobby, and my favorite thing in the world. Every teacher saw it and they let me go above and beyond the assignment because they knew it would make me happy. I had been that way ever since kindergarten. I loved everything about school. It was my home away from home. In fifth grade the gifted students had to go in large groups from four or so schools to one school in order to hold our gifted sessions.

(The Gifted Program is a program for children that have a great natural ability for school or special talent.)

At this school we all treated each other really well. No one ever seemed to purposely offend anyone. Looking back, I'm shocked any of them would ever change that. One of the gifted boys I went there with was Ted, and he would adversely affect the rest of my life. He would recruit other boys from this group and they would join in the harassment.

They took away the happiness school once brought me. They took it all away, and I was left with a lifelong haunting of what they did to me. This is how it happened.

THE BEGINNING
OF THE
END

It started out how one would predict a typical bullying scenario would: teasing about odd habits, finding people to help pick on the victim, trying to find their Achilles' heel, anything to take them permanently out of the game.

Climax: Thirteen-year-old female on heart monitor heads to emergency room because of severe convulsions that resemble full body seizures, and will, in time, be accompanied by brain and heart pains and vivid hallucinations. As her symptoms worsen over time, a local psychiatrist suggests she receive in-house treatment in a treatment facility in another city.

✡ ✡ ✡

SIXTH GRADE

I look up to my brother. I happen to like what he likes. He enjoys being that different guy everybody knows. I believe I can express myself this way too. Can I?

Hair color and nail color seem to be the most easily changeable things about your physical outlook especially for eleven-year-old girls, but should simple physical characteristics give others the right to degrade you? I always told people it didn't matter. To some people it does matter. To some people it matters enough to torment you every time they get the chance to.

Someone, whom we'll call Ted, decided that since I decided to dye my hair black and paint my nails black that was my invitation to him and his friends to constantly bully me. Ted called me names like emo and gothic. He told me I shouldn't dress the way I did and shouldn't talk the way I talked. He taught me the feeling behind the word "insecure."

Many of you are probably thinking, "This isn't bad; I have been treated far worse than this." or "This isn't anything serious." But when faced with it five days a week every week when school is in *session, it can add up fast. As it added up, my ways of trying to deal with it added up along with it. They were:*

1. *Ask them to stop.*
2. *Ignore them so they will go away or stop.*
3. *Tell an authoritative figure (e.g. teacher).*
4. *Repeat steps one and two.*
5. *Cry self to sleep at night wondering, "Why only me?"*
6. *Inflict physical harm to my body (e.g. cutting)*

At number six, some of you may gasp while others recognize it as a common way kids scream for attention. I was not screaming for attention. I hid the marks in the best ways possible. No one knew I hurt myself. So when I would go back to school and Ted and his friends would make me feel like the most death-deserving person on the planet, I would temporarily relieve the pain in an unhealthy manner—6. Physical harm to the body Luckily, I hid the worse cuts well enough so no one would think anything of a cut or two on my legs; I was clumsy after all.

I tried everything I thought could help stop all of this from continuing. I began to dread gifted class projects because of the chance we would be paired together. I was stuck in a whirl-pool of whys? Why me? Why would you do that to someone? Why won't he stop? Why can't I stop these feelings of depression? Why can no one see that this is happening right in front of them?

He made me hate my favorite class. He made me feel uneasy about anything I said or did when he was around. I knew if I gave him any more reasons to bully me he would fly with it and the bullying would never end. What insignificant action I did or opinion I had would be the thing to make this year a never-ending downward spiral? Would it be a project I did too well on, the color of nail polish I picked out the night before, or something even pettier? The answer: all of the above.

....

THE START OF SOMETHING NEW

I remember the first time that his words cut so deeply that the only thing I knew could take away the pain would be to cut into myself just as deeply. The minutes before cutting were full of adrenaline, hate, and spite. I knew that it wouldn't solve anything, but I just dreamed and hoped that it would help make it all that much more bearable. Holding the razor, I watched my hand tremble as I started to feel the stinging burning sensation. At first it's just like a paper cut, but then all the things he said to me flooded my body and my hand slipped making the paper cut into a long slit behind my knee. The blood started to leak slowly then, but, no matter what I did, the blood wouldn't stop.

It was in that moment that I finally felt control over my life again. I had the control to end the pain, live with the pain, and survive all because of inflicting bodily harm to myself. Later that night, I couldn't believe I had done what I did. A year earlier I never would have given that a thought—not to mention a second thought and then actually doing it. I felt my life changing and knew I was going to have to find a way to fix it. How long would it take to fix my life so I wouldn't have to hurt myself in order to free myself? *Years.*

BROKEN PROMISES

Later that year, I tried to flatter him out of making fun of me. Obviously, that didn't work. We were doing a class project in gifted on Greek gods. I was doing my project on Aphrodite and Ted was doing his on Hephaestus. Coincidently, Aphrodite was married off to Hephaestus. So, our projects both included one another's topics. We even worked out an agreement that I would mention his god and make Hephaestus sound really good, and then he would stop being mean to me all the time. Well, I talked about his god in my presentation and mentioned how well Ted described Hephaestus in comparison to the aspect of my research that included him. He shook his head okay when I was finished with my report, and I felt this huge weight being lifted from my shoulders. Finally, I had found a way to stop Ted. Hadn't I?

No, I hadn't. He went back on his word and the very next day was back to being rude to me. It got worse from that point on. He knew I was trying my hardest to make it stop, and that made him try and hurt me even worse. This was where I realized it was going to take much more to stop him. I regained the weight of the world and with it a thousand more insecurities.

HIDING FROM THE WORLD

The gifted kids went on a field trip to the community college every year. Normally, this would be one of the most fun times of the year. Ted was gifted though; he went on the field trip, too. As I was about to walk to my next class at the college, he offered to walk me there because he had a class in the same building. I was shocked but hoped that this could act as a way we could let everything go and start anew. We talked about the weather and which classes had been fun. He was like an entirely different person. As we got to the building I turned to tell him it was nice talking to him, but then I froze. He looked at me and acted like he was slitting his wrists. He stared me straight in the eyes with the most maniacal smile I had ever seen in my life. I was frozen with emotion as I flashed back and saw myself cutting in the bathtub, watching the blood run down the drain slowly. I came to my senses and turned and walk away; so did he. He didn't have a class in my building; his was in the opposite direction. He went through all of that just to hurt me.

I couldn't wait to get home. I was a zombie for the rest of the day. When I got on the school bus to go home, I couldn't help but let a few tears escape. I was ready to explode, but, luckily, my stop was the first stop on the way home. I ran off the bus and started hysterically crying. This would never go away. I couldn't believe how much pain I was in. I ran home but didn't even stop to go inside. I went through our side gate and ran to my dad's dog, Sheeba. I buried my face in her side and wept until twenty minutes later when my mom came outside freaking out. She had no idea where I had been. I didn't use my key to unlock the doors so she knew I wasn't in the house. I didn't have any friends nearby so there was no place I could be. She had already called the school asking about the buses and if there had been any problems reported.

I couldn't believe she cared so much. I had hurt her, but, in doing so, I wouldn't have to hurt myself that night. I worried her, but I realized how much my mom really did love me. Maybe Ted was wrong; maybe I was still supposed to be alive.

Sixth grade was where it all began. Believe it or not, it was also probably the year Ted did the least amount of emotionally damaging harassment. It was also the year that I did the least amount of physical harm to my body since the bullying began. You'll see that in the next couple of years I took some different directions to trying to deal with Ted. Unfortunately, number six on the list stayed, and only intensified from there on out.

....

SUMMERTIME

Would summer really replace school as my new haven?

With Ted out of my life I hoped I would be able to have a happy, fun summer. To most people it would look as if summer really was all I hoped it would be, but it was all smoke and mirrors. His harsh words haunted me even in the happiest times. But how do you tell your parents you want to die? How can they understand that the mere words of a boy have made me inflict bodily harm to myself? I didn't know how to tell them, so I began to leave breadcrumb hints in my actions, words, and writing. Unfortunately, my façade of a happy-go-lucky girl was portrayed vividly well. As sure as the sun rises in the east, I would find a comfort in my razor for many more years.

SEVENTH GRADE

If you can't beat them, join them.

That was my motto going into the seventh grade. I hoped that after racking my brain all summer, this would be an effective way to end the harassment. I tried very hard to befriend Ted and his friends. No, that didn't mean I was about to help inflict the kind of emotional pain I was dealing with on some other helpless victim. Soon, I found that there was a simple mathematical answer to that.

Me + Ted + Ted's friends = Error

But

Me + my best work + my best work extended to doing the work of Ted and his friends in group projects = Ted and his cronies happy and them backing off for a short period of time

That short period of time—usually a week— was when my hell became my haven again. But Group projects will only carry a girl so far. As the harassment went deeper, so did my razor.

If I Could Have Any Superpower It Would Have Been Invisibility.

I had this blue jacket. It became one of the most sentimental possessions I owned. It was a part of me starting in seventh grade. I wore it every day; rain or shine. Whether it was 28° or 101°, it didn't matter because the jacket was my safety blanket. I began to hide behind it. When I realized I could hide behind a jacket, I started looking for other things I could use as safety blankets.

My bangs were the next safety blanket. People always got upset with me for hiding my face behind my bangs, but what none of them knew was that it was keeping me that much more sane. Hiding behind my bangs and jacket helped me try to become invisible.

All I wanted was to be able to shrink away. I pined to be invisible. I wanted to be the nothing that Ted made me feel like I was. At least then I wouldn't feel the need to hurt myself. Then I would fit into the mold I was supposed to, right? But did a mold exist for "nothing"?

The answer: no, it does not.

STRIKE ONE AT MY ACHILLES' HEEL

Ted actually began to sabotage my schoolwork. In our gifted history class he would send people over—or do it himself—to mess up my timed assignments so that I wasn't the first to finish. It was important to me to always achieve the absolute best grade that I could;

I would practice and practice for assignments and he would ruin them. I felt completely stripped of my passion. I was so mad. I had to keep moving Ted's cronies away from my projects just to be able to finish. How could that happen time after time and the teacher not do anything about it? What's a girl to do when the one thing she is good at is under attack? How many more things would he take away from me?

Resorting to number six was my only way to deal with it.

Another time we did a group project together. I was ready to do all the work because I already knew him and the others would just rely on me to do it all because I wouldn't fail. I was in charge of making the model and him and two others were in charge of writing an essay; one lousy essay was all I asked of them. I prepared the two and-a-half-feet-by-three-feet adobe pueblo. The Styrofoam boards were covered in Plaster of Paris and colored to look like the stucco on an old adobe home. There were multiple houses with doors and windows. I even hung red chili peppers outside the doors. There were tiny bowls of cornmeal and pottery. It was all laid out on a wooden plank covered in glue then dusted with sand. It looked like the real deal. In other words, an automatic "A" as long as the others did their part.

They didn't do their part. I freaked out and started writing the essay. Unfortunately, I didn't get very far on the essay, and by "not very far" I mean I had half a paragraph and then our team was up for our presentation. I looked at Ted and he smiled knowing I was ready to break down within seconds of the start of our presentation. I positioned the adobe so everyone could see it very clearly and started to explain why I had what I had on there and the steps I took to make it.

I looked at our teacher and was ready to throw up. She wanted to hear about the essay or for us to read the essay. Ted grabbed my paper with half a paragraph and started to read it and then made a big show of saying, "the end." I wanted to cry. The teacher was furious and Ted just kept smiling at me. He knew he was breaking me down and that I was ready to fall to pieces. I fell into a chair and looked down at the floor until the teacher called me up to her desk. She asked me what happened and I started to explain; I couldn't write the essay because I did the entire model by myself. She realized what had happened and didn't penalize me for what they did. What they really did, however, was get under my skin. Ted was taking away my schoolwork, and that was the only thing I really thought that I was good at.

....

STRIKE TWO

When Ted's tormenting was especially rough on any specific day I tried to find solitude in my dad's dog, Sheeba. Normally, this wouldn't be enough and I would have to cut myself, even if it was just a bit. A day when I could pet Sheeba and feel the tiniest bit better about life was determined a good day.

Unfortunately, Sheeba was getting on in years. One day—a particularly bad day—I came home and my parents gave me the news that they had had to put Sheeba down that morning. I knew it was coming but it still hurt so much.

The next day at school I was sitting in my English class and I overheard my teacher and Ted say, *"The dog is dead. Indeed, the dog is dead."* They were, of course, not talking about my dog, but about our pencil holder dog in the class; it was dead because it had no pencils. But it brought on the emotional fireworks anyway.

Note: Two other girls in that class had shed some tears on lost dogs earlier that year so this should have been relatively acceptable. It was acceptable for them to cry; why not me? "Well, I'm sure it was acceptable," is probably what you're thinking, but you must keep in mind that I had Ted as a tormentor. I left class until I felt more composed and returned to finish my test.

Days, weeks, months, even a year later and this day was still brought up. Ted would come up to me and ask:

"Hey, how's Sheeba doing?"

"Hey Brandy, how's the dog? Oh wait, she died, didn't she? Oh well."

"Brandy, your dog died. Just making sure you remember."

"Brandy, do you remember in Mrs. So-and-So's class when I made you cry? That was so funny."

These comments burned with the best of them. I could not fathom that he would actually resort to bringing up my pet that had died. Then he even had the audacity to believe it was him that made me cry, not just the mere loss of the pet. Well, there goes more power to his, unfortunately, already swollen head.

STRIKE THREE AND I WAS READY TO BE OUT

All of these new ways of hurting me combined with the old made me dread school every single day. I would literally worry myself sick about having to see him each day. Almost every day for the whole seventh grade year I threw up each morning before school. At the time I didn't realize that it could be a sign of how much stress I was really under. Everyone just thought I had a weak immune system and was getting sick. Everyone, that is, except for Ted.

This became just one more thing he would be able to hit me with. Kids at school knew I was sick because I would feel terrible all the time because of throwing up in the mornings. You could see it on my face, and no one misread it for anything but a stomach bug until Ted had his say in the matter. Without knowing it, I had developed a very bad case of bulimia. At least that is what you would hear from Ted in the lunchroom, outside, even whispered in classes. I cannot express to you how many kids that year, some of whom I didn't even know, came up to me and asked me if it was true I was bulimic. I was not only all these other things Ted accused me of being, but now I had supposedly developed an actual disorder too. I hated having to explain myself to all those people. I felt like it was a sign from him and everyone else telling me I *needed* to be bulimic because I was too big. There you go, Ted, one more way you were able to tear my image of myself down even lower.

For those of you out there wondering, I never was bulimic. I would never consider throwing up to make myself skinny. Mainly, this is because I hate throwing up more than your average person.

AN ATTEMPT AT REVEALING REALITY

An Inside Battle
The strokes of the brush
The marks left from the bristles
The swirls and twists
The red streaks
Cut through the paper.
The yellow battles
With the red.
The colors blaze.
The wet flames
Form on the paper.
Time passes.
The flames dry.
But
The battles continues
Although the blaze
Seems to slowly
Fade.

This was one of my attempts to show my English teacher that I needed help. I wanted help. I was trying to show that I was purposely hurting myself, and I wanted to stop. This was not my first attempt at trying to show her and it was not my last. Our class was big on poetry, especially on hiding messages in our poems. I was longing for this metaphor to be the end of all the self-mutilation. I was the painting, and my life was what was fading.

Her comments on my poem were as follows:

"Good title! Nice ending.

Brandy, your poem is lovely! A word painting! Keep writing!"

I wanted to scream. I wanted to ask **why**.

Why don't you see what I am trying to tell you? I feel like dying is my only choice, but I'm truly trying to look for alternatives.

The night I received her feedback my mind was in a wind tunnel going in only one direction—and that was south. I couldn't stop thinking about how painful it was to attend school every day. I despised the way I was treated and could not find a possible solution. No action was taken to assure that I was safe at school. I pleaded with my English teacher through my poetry for her to help me. Nothing ever changed. Now, I guess I can't blame her for not noticing; I never told her outright that I was suicidal because I was not strong enough at the time to do so. But shouldn't she have seen what was right in front of her?

That night I had made up my mind; I was committing suicide. Only by doing that could I stop all the torture I was going through.

My family has a medicine cabinet. My dad has diabetes, high blood pressure, my siblings never finished their antibiotics, and we always had plenty of Tylenol and ibuprofen in the house. I grabbed a bit of each of them. I had my water ready. I felt a sudden ease swallow me just as I was about to swallow these pills. My pills touched my lips and I parted my mouth.

The phone rang.

It was my dad.

He was calling to see how my day went and telling me to take out the trash—go figure.

I was about to take out the biggest piece of trash I could—me.

I told him a quick "Fine" and got off the phone as quickly as possible. I collapsed on the cold, hard kitchen floor and started to cry. At that moment in time, I could not end my life. I placed the pills back in their bottles and decided a big helping of self-mutilation would have to suffice for tonight. I cut my ankles, cut the back of my knee, and watched the blood mix with the water making swirls and twists inside the tub. Sudden serenity washed over me. For this moment Ted could not decide anything for me. I was in control. Regrettably, that moment of ease only lasted so long.

....

CURIOSITY ALMOST KILLED THE CAT

Things went from really bad to even worse after that. A month or two later Ted's bullying was just too much. I wanted to show him how much he hurt me. I wanted to hurt him as much as he hurt me. I wrote him a note. I rewrote it many times, asking if this is what Ted wanted, if this was what I was supposed to do. I wondered if

I was supposed to be understanding or angry. Finally, I decided on angry and the note went something along the lines of this:

Ted, I have finally made you happy.

I did what you wanted.

I have killed myself, and it is entirely your fault.

You drove me to this.

Love, Brandy

I folded up this note and stuck it in my pocket. That night when my dad came home from work I would ask him to help me with the final technicalities of suicide. He had been a Boy Scout leader and knew the different types of knots including the hangman's knot. I was a curious girl, and he knew this really well. I sat next to him on the couch after dinner. All the while the note was burning a hole in my back pocket.

"Dad, can you show me how to tie a hangman's knot?"

"Sure, baby girl. Let's go out to the shop."

That was all it took. Now, don't start thinking my dad is a poor father because he isn't. This wasn't the first time I had asked him to show me something because I read about it in a book. This was not his fault. It was my doing. We went out to our woodworking shop in the backyard and he took out a piece of rope. He showed me how to tie a noose. My plan could be fulfilled. *Not.*

The rope was too short. I wouldn't be able to use it to kill myself. I had been planning on putting the note at my feet when I hung myself that next day after school. When they found me they would find the note and the reason why I killed myself.

I took the trash out to the dumpster that night. After I threw the trash in I took a long hard look at the note I wrote. I crumpled it up and threw it in the dumpster.

....

FINAL ATTEMPT AT SEEKING HELP IN SEVENTH GRADE

I continued on trying to find ways to make Ted stop. At the end of the school year in that same English teacher's class, we were reading our version of what would have happened later in a story we had read earlier that year. I didn't want to read mine because I had used the assignment as another attempt at reaching out for help. I told her I thought it didn't need to be read, but she insisted someone read it whether it was me, a classmate, or herself. Guess who volunteered to read it for me?

Ted sat on a stool and read about how this little girl was driven insane because of a traumatic experience. As he read it I started praying he would see the connection. I even used his favorite word, *haven*.

If only he had asked me why I chose that to happen, if only the teacher or one of my peers had noticed how I was exactly like the little girl, and if only I had conjured up enough will to be able to say those five words—I don't want to live. But none of those events happened and so my story continued on to the summer after seventh grade. I was being driven mad, insane, crazy, and ill because of the words from some stupid boy. I was watching my life unravel as I felt my will to live fade away. I just wanted someone to see my pain and reach out to me. No one reached out to me, and I was left to my own devices in order to keep going.

I wish I could let you see the words I wrote out. I wish I could show you how loudly I screamed of a tortured soul. But I can't show you those words. I tore up that page years later, hoping that one day memories of that day would no longer haunt me.

SUMMER AFTER SEVENTH GRADE

It invades every crevice of my life.

Like the summer before, I had hoped the school break would ease some pain and I could, for the time being, forget all about Ted, but again I was incorrect. I still heard his voice whispering in my head. I still fell into the victim role of this never ending torture. One day, my brother called out and said I had some people at the door. Normally, you would think, "Okay, no big deal." Wrong! It was a huge deal. This would be a major, epic event. I wasn't like my brother who was always having a friend coming by the house. I went to friends; none lived close enough by me to walk.

Who was at the door? A boy I went to school with that lived down the block and Ted were standing outside my house. I went out and tried to hide every ounce of my fear. I talked to them for a good fifteen minutes before I went inside.

My entire body was quaking in his wake. He had finally invaded every space I had. He took away my last safe house and smashed it under his stupid Nike shoes. He made only one comment directed at my self-esteem that day, but it was enough. Enough to tear away the last shred of hope I thought I had. I no longer could leave school thinking no more Ted. He knew where I lived, and he could use that to his advantage.

It was the only time he came to my house, luckily, but that summer I saw him more than I would have liked. He started to hang around my friend's house. She was one of my closest friends. Later on in the summer they started to have that summer fling everyone has at some point in their life. For her, it was one of the best summers of her life. For me, it was the summer where I couldn't hide from those who tore me apart. I took refuge in her house at times when my depression got so bad that I just needed her at my side. Unfortunately, Ted invaded that area too and the snide remarks from school were still directed at me. Everyone, excluding Ted and I, just ignored them.

I wish I could have ignored them too.

EIGHTH GRADE

BIG DOGS ON CAMPUS

Ha, not the kids I was going to school with. They were still the same on the inside even if they had grown four inches over summer or dyed their hair or lost fifteen pounds or all of the above. These were the same people no matter what grade you stuck them in. The only real difference was that they got meaner as they got older.

I really grew to hate parts of eighth grade. Ted became more than I ever feared he would become. When I saw him, I lost all sight of why I was alive. He finally had complete control even if he didn't fully realize it. His words tore me apart. As if this wasn't enough, he decided to officially enlist the help of four other boys in our grade that also happened to share most of our classes. He had sought their help individually over the years, but it was this year that they would all come at me with their harsh words and actions all at once. It is harder when it's one against five—so much harder.

When you have five people coming at you with insults of every kind five days a week for seven hours each day you are bound to be affected by it. I had already been affected by just Ted, but when we add his cronies it made everything ten times worse. These were the people I had, in years past, considered my friends. Now, they were telling me I had no reason to live. They told me these things day after day. To them I was nothing more than the dirt beneath them.

"Why don't you just go and kill yourself?" *I ask myself the same thing every day.*

"Hey, Brandy, can I see your wrists where you cut!" *If only they knew I cut on my ankles and legs.*

"Are you going to go home and hang yourself today?" *Unfortunately, that has already failed me.*

"Aw, are you going to go home and cut yourself?" *I wish the "aw" was sincere instead of sarcastic.*

Last but not least, "When are you going to commit suicide, Brandy?" *I don't know, but will any of you care in the least bit when I do?*

....

WHICH IS WORSE: A TEACHER WHO BULLIES A STUDENT OR A TEACHER WHO SEES A STUDENT BEING BULLIED AND DOES NOTHING ABOUT IT?

I had a teacher who was like another mom to me. She was funny, nice, and a really good teacher. I told her really **almost** everything. I told her when I was having problems with friends, teachers, family, and even boyfriends.

Note: I hate that I have to write the words I'm about to write, but I feel I have to be completely honest in order for this book to do as much good as it can.

I even told her directly that Ted teased me and it was really hurting me. She knew I was being bullied but didn't do anything about it. Yes, she told him to stop. But does that count if he doesn't? Does it count if, even after being told, she sees it and lets it all go? Since when is bullying dismissible, unimportant, and not worth a trip to the principal's office? The boys did it in her class. One day it got so bad that my heart was racing, the tears were ready to burst forward, and I couldn't take it anymore. I screamed at them to shut up and stop it. If anyone had any doubt in their mind about how much pain they were putting me through it would all have ended right then and there. The teacher didn't do anything to back up what I had said. The thing that makes this all worse is that she was supposed to be the teacher in charge of stopping bullying throughout my middle school, and she couldn't even stop it in her own classroom.

Also, that year a few of the boys and I shared one particular teacher who was almost as bad as Ted. No, she didn't tell me to go kill myself or that I wasn't worth the air I breathed, but she did pick on me. I have a stuttering problem and when I get nervous it gets worse. Whenever she had me read in class I always felt this immense pressure like I was trying to escape from something terrible. She would make fun of my stuttering and have half the class laughing hysterically while the other half was either stunned or trying not to be noticed. I wasn't the only student she had picked on. I was, however, the only student who went on to stand up for the other kids because I couldn't stand to see someone be put in the position I was in. The worst part was that by her doing it, it showed the boys bullying is okay.

Note to teachers: it is not okay at all. Ever. No matter the circumstances.

....

RUNNING OUT OF OPTIONS

Near the beginning of eighth grade I was ready to burst from all of the pain. I just wanted out of it, but I didn't want to have to kill myself unless that was my only viable option left. I wanted to leave. I wanted to run away and go so far that I wouldn't ever have to worry about running into Ted ever again.

I started to make a plan about how I could run away. Yes, I know every kid wants to run away at some time in their youth, but I didn't see it as running away exactly. I saw it as running towards a life free of the pain I'd known for almost three years at that point. I wanted a chance to live life, not merely survive it. I was hardly surviving and I wanted so much more. I wanted to live a carefree childhood where worrying about how deep I had to cut that night wasn't something that crossed my mind. I wanted a childhood where the life I had matched the life everyone thought I had.

My problem was I didn't know how to run away. I realized that being alive without my family was worse than being dead because then I would miss them. I knew I wouldn't be able to survive if I were to run away and at least, at that point, I was still surviving. I made a vow that day, though, that one day I would leave and be able to live the life I've always wanted.

The life I wanted is no longer the life I wish to have. I wanted to never have to think about the pain Ted caused me. I kept thinking if only I could forget then maybe all my pain would go away. Now I thrive on what I have become since then. Each day I grow and realize how much strength I had when I was able to put down the razor. I was able to stop. Now, because of that I have the chance to be there to stop others from making the mistake I tried to make so many times.

A PUPPET SHOW ALL MY OWN

The boys continued the abuse and added more ways to show my lack of worth. They started doing hand movements that almost looked as if they were putting on a hand play. The catch was that the play always had the same plot and lead. I was the lead, and I would commit suicide in either of one of two forms: hanging myself or jumping off a building. They would tear strings from their clothes and tie it in a loop to emphasize the noose. This may sound childish to you, silly, and like it should have had no reason to impact me the way it did. Well, if they had done it once or twice, it may not have made me feel so low. That was not the case. They did it every school day, multiple times a day.

Miming me jumping off a building would haunt me in my sleep for years to come. Miming me hanging myself stung more than they would ever realize since it had been a plan of mine that just wasn't fulfilled.

WHEN ALONE WITH MY THOUGHTS THEY BECOME DEMONS

I cut myself the worst in eighth grade. I was taking a bath and I couldn't stop crying. I wanted to die right there in the warm water that was surrounding me. The seed they had planted kept egging me on by telling me how warm the water was, how it would be a peaceful way to leave this world. The inner voice I have had all my life was begging me not to do it, not today. They both kept at it to the point that I didn't know which one I wanted. Did I want to die and leave all this pain? Yes. Did I want to be able to live a full life filled with happiness? Yes.

I compromised with them both. I cut and slit, and I watched the blood seep into the water. I thought it was beautiful. I was able to capture the beauty of pain right there. I felt power in being able to control the amount of pain I was feeling. After the water started to turn color near my legs I got up and washed off. Just like nothing had happened. I ran the water over the cuts and applied pressure to make it stop. I was able to get out of the bathroom and feel free one more time. I had a total of ten cuts on my legs, but lucky for me no one would ever see because it was December and I had pants on all the time.

···

THE UNFORTUNATE NIGHTLY RITUALS

To put myself to bed most nights I would have to cry myself to sleep. Night after night I cried into my pillow wishing I was someone else, somewhere else. If I could only be like So-And-So then Ted wouldn't hurt me the way he does. If only my parents had stayed in Massachusetts, maybe I would have never met Ted in the first place. If I looked more like my big sister everyone would like me more and no one would dare bully me. If only I had my brothers' personalities then maybe I would have the guts to find some clever way to make them realize how wrong they were. I thought of myself as one big mistake. If all these kids believed I wasn't supposed to be alive any longer, who's to say they're wrong? What made their opinion about me more accurate than my opinion about myself before their thoughts polluted my soul?

All the pain-filled emotions would get to the point where I was screaming at the top of my lungs—internally when my family was home and externally when they were away. I couldn't imagine my family's reaction to me feeling this way. I didn't know how I would react to one of them saying they felt unworthy of life, so I couldn't let them see how much pain I was in. I wanted them to see it, but I just couldn't let them.

I remember feeling like there would never be an end to any of the pain the boys caused. I lay in my bed at night praying that God would let me never wake up again. I begged and pleaded with him night after night to just end it for me. I would write farewell notes to put under my pillow each night, explaining why I had to leave this world and that I would wait for all of my family and friends in the next. As all the torturing continued my notes became more abrasive.

Why couldn't anyone see the pain I was in? Why did everyone ignore it? You ignored it. You could have stopped this. I hate you all because of what they did. I hate that I had to go through these years of my life alone. I hate that I died alone. I needed to have someone save me from not only them but from myself because of what they turned me into. No one was there to save me. Where are all the real-life superheroes? Why was I the unworthy one?

The death notes were never directed at any one person in particular, but as I continued writing them I realized they were either meant to be to me or to God.

I began to hate myself for not only the things the boys told me, but because I started to believe them as well. I believed the words of these five people instead of listening to the words of all the people I cared about. I was driven on the ideals of others instead of my own. I chose to let their words affect me, but after so many hateful thoughts directed at me it would have been hard for just about anyone to not adopt the mob mindset. I let their thoughts invade my every day, but it was because I couldn't find the strength not to.

I started to doubt there ever was a God in the first place. How could any righteous God condone all of the pain in this world? If he really cared about his children then why wouldn't he stop their pain—my pain? No one could answer those questions for me. I stopped believing in God for a long time. I felt I had no reason left to believe in any kind of higher power. The only question left on my mind was if there is a God would he still help me to walk out of all the darkness that had consumed me after I had turned on him?

....

CORNERED IN LIFE AND CORNERED IN THE CLASSROOM

This title is very self-explanatory. The boys mentally cornered me in a low part of my life and did it physically in the classrooms as well. You ask where the teacher was; I ask myself the same question even though I know the answer. She was behind her desk the whole time.

They would corner me and start acting like they were cutting their wrists. They would do the hand people and hang me and ask me why I was still here. They told me I didn't belong and that I just should go home and die. It was like I was stuck in a tornado seeing everything that was important to me and everything that was meaningful to me leave. All I was left with was the painful emotional words I kept hearing them scream at me.

"You are a cutter; go home and cut and slit your wrists."

"You should just die."

"You are not important anyway."

They told me things like that over and over. And were they really yelling? No. They were saying it just loud enough for me to hear and no one else. They were torturing me, and there were almost ten other people in the room who had absolutely no idea about any of it. I broke away from the pack of animals and went to my desk. I stayed there the rest the class with my head down doing absolutely nothing.

I was completely broken. They had finally done it. I went home that night and slit both ankles and watched the blood ooze out knowing how broken I really was. I watched knowing it wouldn't take much more for me to just finish it. They had tried to break me for years in so many ways and finally they did what they had set out to do. Would this stop them? Of course it wouldn't. It only fed their power knowing that they have accomplished destroying a girl's will to live.

I grew an even stronger façade and pleaded with fate that it would make them stop, show them that they didn't get to me, show them everything that they thought was true was the opposite, and maybe they would give everything up and realize how painful bullying can be. They didn't realize it. They never stopped. I was to forever be their puppet. Either they would make my day not so bad and limit what they said to one or two comments or they would terrorize me to the point that I had to mutilate my body in order to feel in control. I'm at the lowest point over and over. After I reach the bottom I struggle with standing up again. I am constantly trying to face this struggle. I stand up after being knocked down repeatedly. I am learning a new low each and every time. As the pain continues, so does my journey with these lowest points. I hit rock bottom, only to find that there is another rock bottom just waiting to be hit again.

....

PLAY – PAUSE – REWIND – PLAY – PAUSE – REWIND

My days were filled with the same thing over and over and over and over and over and over and over and over and over and over and over and over and over and over and

over and over and over and over and over and
over and over and over and over and over and
over and over and over and over and over and
over and over and over and over and over and
over and over and over and over and over and
over and over and over and over and over and
over and over and over and over and over and
over and over and over and over and over and
over and over and over and over and over and
over and over and over and over and over and
over and over and over and over and over and
over and over and over and over and over and
over and over and over and over and over and
over and over and over and over and over and
over and over and over and over and over and
over and over and over and over and over and
over and over and over and over and over and
over and over and over and over and over and
over and over and over and over and over and
over and over and over and over and over and
over and over and over and over and over and
over and over and over and over and over and
over and over and over and over and over and
over and over and over and over and over and
over and over and over and over and over and
over and over and over and over and over and
over and over and over and over and over and
over and over and over and over and over and
over and over and over and over and over and
over and over and over and over and over and
over and over and over and over and over and

over and over and over and over and over and
over and over and over and over and over and
over and over and over and over and over and
over and over and over and over and over and
over and over and over and over and over and
over and over and over and over and over and
over and over and over and over and over and
over and over and over and over and over and
over and over and over and over and over and
over and over and over and over and over and
over and over and over and over and over and
over and over and over and over and over and
over and over and over and over and over and
over and over and over and over and over and
over and over and over and over and over and
over and over and over and over and over and
over and over and over and over and over and
over and over and over and over and over and
over and over and over and over and over and
again.

....

PLAY — PAUSE — REWIND — PLAY — PAUSE — REWIND

My days were filled with the same thing over
and over and over and over and over and
over and over and over and over and over and
over and over and over and over and over and
over and over and over and over and over and

over and over and over and over and over and
over and over and over and over and over and
over and over and over and over and over and
over and over and over and over and over and
over and over and over and over and over and
over and over and over and over and over and
over and over and over and over and over and
over and over and over and over and over and
over and over and over and over and over and
over and over and over and over and over and
over and over and over and over and over and
over and over and over and over and over and
over and over and over and over and over and
over and over and over and over and over and
over and over and over and over and over and
over and over and over and over and over and
over and over and over and over and over and
over and over and over and over and over and
over and over and over and over and over and
over and over and over and over and over and
over and over and over and over and over and
over and over and over and over and over and
over and over and over and over and over and
over and over and over and over and over and
over and over and over and over and over and
over and over and over and over and over and
over and over and over and over and over and
over and over and over and over and over and
over and over and over and over and over and
over and over and over and over and over and
over and over and over and over and over and
over and over and over and over and over and

over and over and over and over and over and
over and over and over and over and over and
over and over and over and over and over and
over and over and over and over and over and
over and over and over and over and over and
over and over and over and over and over and
over and over and over and over and over and
over and over and over and over and over and
over and over and over and over and over and
over and over and over and over and over and
over and over and over and over and over and
over and over and over and over and over and
over and over and over and over and over and
over and over and over and over and over and
over and over and over and over and over and
over and over and over and over and over and
over and over and over and over and over and
over and over and over and over and over and
again.

....

PLAY — PAUSE — REWIND — PLAY — PAUSE — REWIND

My days were filled with the same thing over and
over and over and over and over and over and
over and over and over and over and over and
over and over and over and over and over and
over and over and over and over and over and
over and over and over and over and over and
over and over and over and over and over and

over and over and over and over and over and
over and over and over and over and over and
over and over and over and over and over and
over and over and over and over and over and
over and over and over and over and over and
over and over and over and over and over and
over and over and over and over and over and
over and over and over and over and over and
over and over and over and over and over and
over and over and over and over and over and
over and over and over and over and over and
over and over and over and over and over and
over and over and over and over and over and
over and over and over and over and over and
over and over and over and over and over and
over and over and over and over and over and
over and over and over and over and over and
over and over and over and over and over and
over and over and over and over and over and
over and over and over and over and over and
over and over and over and over and over and
over and over and over and over and over and
over and over and over and over and over and
over and over and over and over and over and
over and over and over and over and over and
over and over and over and over and over and
over and over and over and over and over and
over and over and over and over and over and
over and over and over and over and over and
over and over and over and over and over and
over and over and over and over and over and

over and over and over and over and over and
over and over and over and over and over and
over and over and over and over and over and
over and over and over and over and over and
over and over and over and over and over and
over and over and over and over and over and
over and over and over and over and over and
over and over and over and over and over and
over and over and over and over and over and
over and over and over and over and over and
over and over and over and over and over and
over and over and over and over and over and
over and over and over and over and over and
over and over and over and over and again.

The hateful words tossed my way never
ended. They multiplied like mad. Each hour was
filled with darkness. I wished to forget for just a
minute that I wasn't supposed to be here still.
The boys wanted me dead so badly. They tortured me. I screamed out in pain in my mind
but even it was shushed by little Teds that had
implanted themselves into my brain. I began to
believe it all. They were brainwashing me into
wanting to kill myself. They made me into what
I became. I was never able to be alone and
be happy. I always had him in my head yelling,
telling me I didn't belong, and telling me I was
nothing. The days ran together, and each day
was the same in the sense that, no matter what,
I would be tormented; I would be picked on. I
would be told that I didn't deserve to breathe

the air I breathe. I had no reason to live anymore. I longed for a blade at all hours of the day and night. I needed to be in control for just that minute because that one minute would let me live for another day. That one minute would let me breathe another breath. It helped me to survive, but the whole time it was killing me too.

A TEST THAT BECAME SO MUCH MORE THAN A TEST

Unfortunately, stressors in my life started to affect my health. I was getting heart palpitations frequently and having bad dizzy spells. The doctors put me on a heart monitor for thirty days. In those next thirty days Ted's bullying became more frequent and so did the heart palpitations. Also, we were going to have school wide testing.

I loved testing. I especially loved Criterion Reference Tests (CRT). Usually, it didn't stress me out whatsoever. I was able, in years past, to be able to block out the world and excel with no hint of the bullying problem that had started in sixth grade. I went over everything twice, and I wrote in every last space possible to fully complete every answer. Naturally, this made me take longer than most everyone else, but the test still didn't stress me out. Eighth grade was an entirely different story. I had the worse stress

I had ever had during a test. The stress came from no other than Ted himself.

Ted and his pals were in the same testing room as me. At the very first break during testing they handed me a paper folded into a tiny square. I didn't want to open it so they opened it in front of me. It was a detailed drawing of me killing myself. It took every ounce of my being to continue testing. Each break they put a drawing on my desk depicting more vivid ways of me dying. The pictures had a range of action in them. I hang myself, shoot myself, cut myself, jump off of a building, and last, but not least, they shoot me. As it moved on to them killing me and me screaming out in pain in the drawings, I started dying more and more on the inside and they were the ones inflicting all the pain. Oh the joy of thought bubbles. They wrote what they thought of me and what they thought I should think of me too. Bottom line: they wanted to break me and I was about to be broken again.

Lucky for me, a very good friend of mine, "Vince," was also in our testing room. As soon as he heard about the drawings he snatched them up and threw them into the trash and told them to never do it again. At that moment, he was truly my hero. He had the strength to stand up to Ted; The strength that I lacked because it had been slowly drained from me over the last three years. Now here was someone who finally took a stand on my behalf. I had someone who cared enough to help. He chose not to ignore the boys. He showed me the true light that still lingered inside the hearts of others. I will never forget his action, and I will never be able to thank him enough. His action—no matter how small it may seem to others—changed my life. Vince gave me hope for the tomorrows in life.

TRYING TO FIND A NICHE

I decided I had wanted to go out for soccer, but you can't play soccer with a heart monitor on. I still wanted to be a part of it so I settled for manager. One day after a particularly brutal Ted day, right before practice my arm started to twitch and move out of control. It became uncontrollable and a new fear wasn't far behind. My mom came to pick me up because I told her I wasn't feeling well. Little did we know my family's life was about to be changed forever.

THE HOSPITAL TRIP THAT BECAME SO MUCH MORE

By the time we got home my whole body was convulsing. I remember walking down the hallway and not being able to make it on my own. Everything was moving. Every limb had developed a mind of its own. My mom called the cardiologist and they sent us to the local emergency room. We went straight there with my dad meeting us in the emergency room parking lot.

My parents had to hold me on either side to get me into the hospital. My legs, arms, and head were all out of my control. The receptionist took one look at me and ran out of her cubicle to put me in a wheel chair. They admitted me faster than we would have ever imagined. Then ran a battery of tests and put me on Valium to control the convulsions. Our family doctor was in the building and said he believed it to be Conversion Disorder (a disorder where your body begins to release stress in a physical manifestation), but if I was his daughter he'd bring me to Albuquerque's emergency room and get an EEG to make sure it wasn't an actual seizure.

They discharged me with a prescription for a Valium-like medicine to help me get through the next day or so. I convulsed throughout the night, and early the next morning we made our way to Albuquerque's Emergency Room. After the three-and-a-half hour drive, we had to wait for eight hours to be seen. When I finally got called they gave me more Valium and it was enough to knock me out. Finally, sleep and a reprieve from all the spasms.

When the doctor came in to talk to me, the truth finally came out. I was out of it, to say the least. She woke me up then she started asking me questions: had I ever hurt myself, did I want to die, had I ever attempted suicide. Her questions rang in my ears. I didn't know what to say. This was the first time anyone had ever directly asked me any of these questions. Silently I thanked whatever was wrong with me, then I cursed it not knowing if they would tell my parents. Uneasily, I told her yes and answered all of her questions. Afterwards she told me I could go to sleep. Full of emotion from telling the truth about the parts she had asked about, I gladly fell asleep.

I never realized how much pain telling the truth could cause until I woke up and saw the look on my father's face. My mother wasn't in the room, but with the emotion his face expressed I didn't think I could handle both of them at once. He started asking me questions while holding back tears, and I started to answer them while holding back tears of my own. I had perfected holding things in and away from my parents, but now that the truth had escaped I faced something even harder. How do you tell your parents—the people that gave you life and cared for you—that you didn't want to be alive anymore, that you were convinced that you had no reason to live? When my mom came in with eyes puffy and red I knew this would just keep getting harder to explain.

I said I told them the truth, but I never said how much of it I could muster.

I didn't say a word about Ted or his friends. I blamed hurting myself on just being sad all the time and not feeling like I was good enough. I kept thinking to myself, "Baby steps, baby steps are what this will take."

The doctors admitted me and I was told to prepare for multiple tests and a lot of waiting. The waiting made the silence between my parents and I weigh down upon us. I sought refuge in having a constant connection with someone back home. Vince was at my side figuratively throughout the entire hospitalization. I spoke with him all day long about the hospital, my fears, and what was going on back home. He called after dinner and his voice helped me find a concrete place to rest. I would fall asleep texting him knowing that no matter what happened in this hospital I would go home to someone that truly cared. I still doubted whether or not I was supposed to be alive, but his being there for me when I felt so lost and alone gave me just a spark of hope that everything would get better—one day.

After the doctors admitted me to the hospital they did the EEG. I felt so lost in that huge hospital. Part of me kept thinking there was no reason to even ask why I hurt myself or what my diagnosis was; I would be gone someday soon anyway. The EEG came back normal and I was sent back to my room. My parents and I were exhausted from everything. All we wanted was sleep and answers. Answers can be harder to come by, so we all settled for sleep.

I slept hoping to hide from all of it only to be awakened by someone who unknowingly would get me through so much. Off in the distance, past the emptiness of my dreams, a voice was beckoning me and I had no strength to do anything but go with it. As I opened my eyes and began making out the soft humming, she turned to me and began singing.

....

WILDFLOWER

She's faced the hardest times you could imagine
And many time her eyes fought back the tears
And when her youthful world was about to fall in
Each time her slender shoulders bore the weight of all
her fears
And a sorrow no one hears still rings in midnight silence
In her ears...

Let her cry, for she's a lady
Let her dream, for she's a child
Let the rain fall down upon her
She's a free and gentle flower growing wild.

And if by chance that I should hold her
Let me hold her for a time
And if allowed but one possession
I would pick her from the garden to be mine.

Be careful how you touch her for she'll awaken
And sleep's the only freedom that she knows
And when you walk into her eyes you won't believe
The way she's always paying for a debt she never owes
And a silent wind still blows that only she can hear
And so she goes...

Let her cry, for she's a lady
Let her dream, for she's a child
Let the rain fall down upon her
She's a free and gentle flower growing wild.

Words by David Richardson. Music by Doug Edwards.
Copyright Edsel Music 1972. Renewed 2000.
Administered worldwide by Nettwerk Songs Publishing.

64

When she was done she took my hand and squeezed, turned to the end of the bed, replaced a trash bag in the can, turned her cleaning cart, and walked out my room but never out of my life. I was beyond speechless. That was the day they discharged me on the condition that in Roswell I have an appointment already scheduled with a psychologist.

If my mother hadn't been awakened by her singing as well, I would have thought she had been an angel sent from God. Later on I would come to realize, wings or no wings, she truly was an angel. I had no idea what song she had sung to me, but I made it my mission to find out once we got out of that place. It was called *Wildflower* by the band Skylark. Now, because of this woman I began to listen to it day in and day out for weeks on end. It kept me going on for weeks.

I started to see a psychologist as soon as we got home. Telling a stranger all my deepest thoughts and feelings turned out to be a whole lot easier than telling those who were closest to me, but even then I couldn't tell all. Eighth grade continued on just as it had left off. The boys were just as intent on making my life hell as they had before.

AN UNKNOWN INTERVENTION

One night when remembering the woman in the hospital proved not enough and I was home alone I cut deeply. I didn't even bother getting in the shower to do it like I normally would. Everything was spinning faster than it ever had. I knew my way around the kitchen and I knew where the knife that would do it best lay. I went and got the knife and stood in the bathroom with it. As I slid down against the door frame thinking about what was in my hand, I looked to the right and I could see on the floor of my room a well-worn piece of paper that had my name on it. It was a note from my best friend who suffers from Cystic Fibrosis. In the note she was telling me when she would be going into the hospital that winter. She unknowingly saved my life. I felt guilt that Ted had enough power to make me believe that my only option left was to kill myself, but she had no control over what was killing her. The CF was taking her life over time and there was nothing she could do about it. I was about to take my own life, but there was something I could do about it. I put the knife back in the kitchen. I couldn't kill myself, not today, not like this, at least not yet.

FINDING A VOICE

We were decorating the gymnasium for our National Junior Honor Society occasion that night when some news traveled throughout the room. News spreads like wildfire in a middle school. One of the boys that tormented me had gotten into a fight. He had lost. I was on the bleachers talking to a friend of mine about it while we waited for the teacher to show up. The boy who had been in the fight heard something I said and yelled at me. All I said was "Did he get punched?" There was no extra enthusiasm in my voice or anything. The boy heard me wrong and started to yell about how I wasn't there so I didn't know what had happened.

That was it. I was not going to let him sit and yell at me, when he tormented me every single day alongside Ted. I went straight up to him and yelled.

"Are you kidding me? You are going to sit here and freak out about what I'm saying about you? News flash: all I said was 'Did he,' meaning you, 'get punched?' I didn't say I wanted you to get hurt, but, you know what, you deserved it. It's called Karma. You sit in class every day and tell me I should go kill myself because I don't deserve to live. You tell me to go home and cut myself because all I'll

ever be is a cutter. Do you even think you can grasp how that makes me feel? I have to deal with you and them every freaking day, but when one person asks a question about you, you flip out and think it's out of line. Well, I'm sorry for asking about your well-being 'Greg.' I promise the next time I won't care enough to ask. You will never understand what you and the boys have done to me."

I stood there, heart pounding, right in front of him and he did nothing. He said nothing. He looked absolutely dumbfounded at the thought that maybe his actions had adversely affected my life. I only screamed the first sentence; after that I spoke very quietly but sternly. This way no one else heard what I was saying, but the one yelled sentence got everyone in the gym's attention and when I turned around almost every single one of them were staring. I had found my voice and had finally admitted to someone how badly they were treating me.

After that, Greg didn't partake in the bullying. I had gotten through to him. It was not enough to make him stick up for me, but I was getting to the point that I might be able to stick up for myself every now and then without having a huge panic attack in the middle of all of it. Could I be making progress?

IS IT THE END OR JUST A START?

The last few weeks of eighth grade are just a blur to me now. All the kids knew I had ended up in the hospital. You would think there would be some sympathy from even the worst tormentors. I wasn't that lucky. They kept on and on with the harsh hand puppets and traumatic teasing. The last day of school we were able to go to any classroom as they were having different types of fun activities in each. To me this was more than finding the best classroom to stay in; it meant I could stay away from Ted, it meant one day of refuge in school. That day I found out Ted was going to the high school across town. At least I ended my middle school experience with hope.

BREAKTHROUGH

The summer between eighth and ninth grade I had the biggest breakthrough and breakdown about everything that had happened to me. I sat one night until three or four in the morning telling my mother all of it. I told her every last detail, explaining about Ted and the pain he caused me. I told her how I hurt myself and why I felt like I had no other option but to do so. Reliving every memory made it all so much worse. I felt the pain as I had whilst it was happening in middle school. I saw the blood I took from my body. I felt the roughness of the rope in my hand. I explained to her that there was no way I could have enough courage to have told them this before, but that I wished that I had. I relived everything and I told everything.

She told me how she wished she had known. She told that if any of the family had just realized it, it all would have stopped a long time ago. I told her it would never have done any good. I told her that some people can't be stopped. I was afraid throughout the whole ordeal that somehow Ted would find me and make me kill myself for telling someone who would listen. We stayed up crying together, yelling together, and finally feeling like I might be able to move on from all of it—together.

Afterward, I went on to tell my big brothers, my big sister, and my dad. I told them each separately everything that I had gone through. I was met by a flood of reactions: anger, sadness, understanding, and so much more. Each reaction was like the one before it, only each exposed their emotions differently. It was like dropping different sized stones in a pond; you will always get the ripples but they come out differently.

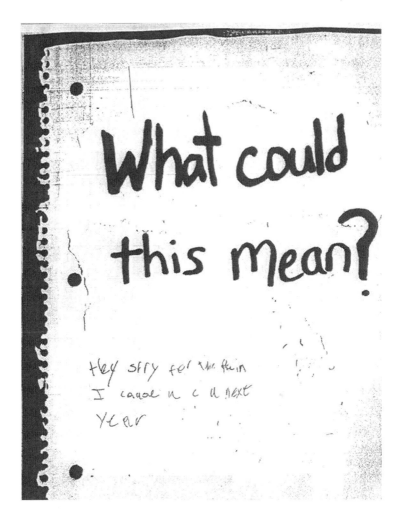

....

AN UNEXPECTED APOLOGY

I found an old notebook when I was cleaning out my room that summer. It was used as a makeshift yearbook in seventh grade because ours came in late that year and we had to pick them up in the summer. Many kids brought spiral notebooks that last day to have everyone sign. Mine got lost for a little while because they started handing it around to a bunch of people. I finally tracked it down and kept a closer watch on it from then on.

The old notebook wasn't something I ever thought would be life changing or eye opening until I found it. I saw on a page near the end the words, "Hey srry for the pain I cause u c u next year." Everyone always signed literally everyone's yearbook. I went through and started comparing handwriting and seeing who had written in my yearbook all three years. There was only one person missing from my makeshift notebook, Ted. The handwriting seemed really similar.

Will I ever know if that was Ted trying to reach out and apologize for his wrongdoings? Could he, too, be a suffering victim that just takes his own pain out on me? Could it be someone else who I have no idea how they could have hurt me? I will never know. But I realized on this day there's a chance that Ted and I may have more in common than I ever imagined.

A WHOLE NEW WORLD—MAYBE

Eighth grade was gone, but the result of Ted and his bullying was just beginning. Luckily, we weren't going to the same high school. I would be free from at least the pack leader though three of the boys were attending the same school I was.

Turns out, I would be free from all of it. Now that the ring leader was gone, all of it was gone. The boys stopped completely when we left middle school. Two of them even apologized and they admitted they only did it because they didn't want to be the next victim for Ted.

Life sure did seem like it would never stay happy for me. The pseudo seizures and other symptoms from the bullying refused to stay away. I was constantly in and out of school because some days the symptoms were just too bad to attend. This was killing me. I loved school so much, and yet, even though he wasn't there Ted was still controlling my life. How long would he be able to control it? How long would I let him?

I had to leave school for most of December my ninth grade year because my anxiety got too bad. Finally, after struggling off and on with it I was put on homebound for the last nine weeks of my freshman year. Homebound was similar to being homeschooled, but was specifically for children with medical problems.

I missed that summer because I had to play catch-up with all of my work from the time I was gone. Homebound was hard not only because I was separated from my peers, losing out on the social experiences you are supposed to have at that age, but I also had difficulty with school. I knew the stuff but at times I wasn't able to write my answers down because of the seizures. My homebound teacher had to resort to giving my tests and homework assignments orally while I was on the floor experiencing all of my symptoms.

I stayed on homebound for the first nine weeks of my tenth grade year as well. When I went back social aspects of school were difficult. People who had stayed in touch with me were different people at school, and I had to find my own new little niche somewhere. Somehow, even with continuing to miss school, I found a place and was able to mark "socially awkward" off my list of character traits—although, from time to time, it still comes back.

My prolonged absences got to the point that my parents and I had decided the best decision for my academic career at that point was to get my GED. As I have described my passion for school earlier I feel the need to say it was purely the lack of attending school that made us come to this conclusion. My grades were still ranked second in my entire class. I was able to keep up with and still succeed in school, but I wasn't attending very often and it became evident that it was in my best interest to bypass the next two years of school and get the GED. So around February the paperwork was drawn up and I had to leave high school. I got my GED and was able to begin online college courses through a local university.

I did encounter a couple new problems, unfortunately, while I was able to attend school. I was harassed by someone who I really didn't even know. He said sexual innuendos and vulgar comments to me. After having dealt with Ted for so long and all the pain he caused me I wasn't going to let this happen without there being a consequence for him. I finally stood up for myself, and then I went straight to a teacher who I was very close to and told her everything that had happened. She then went straight to the vice principal and from there the boy eventually got suspended. I suppose because of the pain Ted caused I was able to have the courage to stop this scumbag from hopefully ever mistreating any other girl the way he mistreated me.

There also was one more incident that really affected me while I was in high school. There was a girl in our gifted class who was really shy and didn't talk much to anyone. She had a quirky, random personality and you just never knew what would come out of her mouth. Overall, I had always thought she was pretty nice. We even attended elementary school together where I had made a point to stick up for her when other kids picked on her. I must say after having the conversation I'm about to relay to you that I wouldn't say I believed in Karma very much.

We were standing around our Common room while waiting for school to begin and she asked me to go over to her. As I walked towards her, I couldn't help but think it was odd that she wanted to talk to me as we hadn't spoken for quite some time. As I arrived at her table she started this conversation:

Girl: "Hey, Brandy. Do you miss middle school?"

Me: "Frankly, no. I don't miss it at all. Why?"

Girl: "Oh, I miss it. I especially miss gifted class. It was always so much fun to watch the boys make fun of you. You always seemed like you were on the verge of tears. *Laughs* It was my favorite part of middle school."

Dumbfounded, fuming, and, most of all, over-whelmingly sad, I walked away from her thinking, "Someone actually saw it and decided to not do anything about it. Not only did they not do anything, they enjoyed watching me hurt. How could anyone ever see someone being tortured and take pleasure in it?" I will never be able to forget the sound of her laughter as I was walking away. I will never be able to understand why someone would admit to seeing all the pain and still choose to do nothing.

....

FINDING THE LIGHT

We lived in a tight knit little neighborhood where if someone comes over and asks you for a cup of sugar, it's not the weirdest thing. Our family was particularly close to one small family, just husband and wife. I always loved them as another uncle and aunt whom I could always rely upon. Never did I know just how much they loved me too. He never believed in a higher power but she did. This didn't drive a wedge between them because they were able to see past it because their love was strong.

When things got particularly rough, many people were praying for answers for me, and I thank you all for every one of those prayers. I do believe they have helped even if in the past I didn't understand. One prayer was different. One prayer made me realize how much each prayer meant.

Back when I was in ninth grade, my dad was typing away on the computer, working, and writing e-mails. I was in the living room lying on the couch. I still remember the thoughts I was having before he called me into the den.

Why do people pray? No one ever gets answers. People die and people get hurt. They lie, steal, and cheat. Is that really a world where an almighty savior controls? I wouldn't think so. How are we supposed to learn how to pray? What is okay to pray for? Tests, crushes, illnesses, deaths, and job interviews are all things I've heard people pray about. If we pray for so many things, does that take away each prayer's importance?

My thoughts were interrupted by my dad telling me to come into the den to look at something. His e-mail was up and he said to read the open message. As I read it I didn't understand it at all. It was an e-mail from that neighbor I considered to be an uncle. Their conversation was talking about how I kept getting sicker and how everyone was really worried. Then I read the words, "I pray every day for her." I didn't understand because he didn't believe in God, but because of me he was praying. I meant enough for someone to change his religious views if it meant it would help me. There had to be a God if he had someone pray for me who hadn't even believed in him before.

I started to realize praying is praying. It doesn't have any boundaries because our God loves every one of us. There isn't a boundary between who he does and does not love. People make mistakes, but that doesn't mean he will damn us to some form of a hell. It was like I had stepped from dry land to under a waterfall. I couldn't believe it. All those people praying for me, and I never knew how much it meant until that day. After I talked to my dad about it I went to my bedroom and I prayed for all those people who had ever said a prayer for me. As I was just about to finish, I said one last prayer for Ted.

Lord, please save his lost soul. I don't think he understands how much he has hurt me or anyone else he has bullied, but even if he does know and doesn't care he still deserves to be saved because your love has no boundaries.

AFTERMATH

AT THE CORNER OF ACTIONS AND REACTIONS

While out in public I was still paranoid about seeing Ted and anyone else who had bullied me in middle school. I was truly horrified at the idea of seeing him after everything that had happened. I was afraid that as I saw him everything he had ever done would wash over me and I would break down right there. I have worried for the last three years every time I go into a store that he will be there. I worried he would come into my work.

I worry to this day about avoiding him to the point that I refuse to go into his work now. I would rather have to shop somewhere else than worry about seeing him and having to be reminded of all the pain he caused me and, most importantly, how little he cares about the pain he caused me.

I continued to see a psychologist and/or psychiatrist every month. I have been through more medical tests and more medication combinations than I could ever count. I may have to continue to be on medication for the rest of my life now because of how traumatic the bullying became. My symptoms of Post-Traumatic Stress Disorder include the following:

- Pseudo seizures that can consist of temporary loss of vision, full body convulsions, and passing out without breathing. These all can be strenuous on my body, and I will never forget how I felt the first time each of them happened.

The first time I lost my vision I had just gotten out of the shower and was walking towards my room. All of a sudden, I lost my balance and everything went black.

I was lying on the floor, and, instantly, I began hysterically crying because I thought I had really just gone blind. My dad came running, asking me over and over what was wrong. Somehow I was able to mumble out that I couldn't see anymore. This all happened within a matter of seconds. It lasted for about twenty seconds and then my vision came back. Those were some of the longest seconds I have ever experienced.

My convulsions worsened in time. In the beginning, my mom could hold me down to protect me against hitting something and breaking it or hurting myself. As time progressed, my spasms became so intense that it took my brother-in-law, my brother, and my father—three grown men—to hold me down.

When I passed out for the first time I didn't understand what had happened. I just remember waking up and seeing my family staring at me wide-eyed and worried. My blackouts would happen in either little bursts wherein I would be out for fifteen seconds, wake up, gasp for breath, and be out again, or I would be out for a little over a minute straight. By the time these started happening I just knew to roll with it. No matter what was happening my family and I just had to find a way to manage it. My family eventually tried many things to wake me up from blackouts: shaking me, yelling, pinching, and even throwing ice cold water on me. None of these ever brought me out of it faster. This has become the most inhibiting of all my symptoms.

- Spontaneous pain in both my head and heart. These pains can become so excruciating at times I will literally scream out in pain. I always try to not let them get to me too badly, but at times there is nothing I can do about it.

- Pseudo hallucinations. These are the worst, emotionally heart wrenching of all my symptoms.. They aren't just any random hallucination. They all stick with the same theme. I see myself dead after having committed suicide.

I have seen myself after being hanged. I have seen myself dripping wet with blood coming from my wrists and engulfing my hands. I have seen myself holding three empty pill bottles. I have seen myself with a slit throat. I have seen myself with a bullet hole in my head, and in another one there is a bullet hole in my chest. I have seen myself so mutilated my only guess is that I jumped into oncoming traffic or something to that effect where I'm hardly recognizable.

The hallucinations last from two seconds to five seconds with the exception of one in particular. In my longest hallucination I saw myself as a younger girl. She was right by my bedside and was handing me a knife with her eyes begging me to take it. She wouldn't go away no matter how hard I tried to make her. I was frozen with fear after that. She lasted about ten seconds, possibly more. For those ten seconds I really thought I needed to do what she wanted because she seemed so uncontrollably sad. It was like my killing myself would be her only way out.

✲ ✲ ✲

Here are a few tests treatments I had to go through throughout this experience of trying to find what was wrong with me.

EKG
EEG
ECG
Tilt Table Test
CAT scan

MRI
Sleep study
Medications
Hypnosis
Lab work
Counseling by psychiatrist
Counseling by psychologist

And here are a few of the medications I was put on with different combinations and dosages throughout this experience.

Depakote
Clonidine
Trazodone
Ketoconazole
Gabapentin
Risperdal
Clomipramine
Klonopin
Lorazepam
Nefazodone
Lunesta
Orap
Cogentin
Haloperidol
Keppra
Temazepam
Trileptal
Propranolol
Lexapro

Aripiprazole
Lithium
Seroquel

All of this only lead to numerous theories and diagnoses. I cannot express to you how much frustration and stress came from the unknown possibilities of what made me sick when all the while what made me sick was Ted. The suffering I had to endure led to physically making me ill with the numerous, previously mentioned symptoms.

REASONS BEHIND THE WORDS

I had to lose out on a lot of things everyone should experience as a child and teen. Luckily, I have been able to see past those losses and grow.

I have already attempted to help end bullying right in my hometown by speaking to all the principals in the district and several of the middle schools as well as elementary schools. I feel like it is needed for teachers and staff to be able to have some form of a reference with kids. They need to be able to have the background knowledge of a teen that has recently experienced bullying within their own school district. As I began to explain about Ted and the hardships I had to face and will continue to face because of his bullying I began to see a flicker of the significance I could have on these people. In their faces I read an understanding. The understanding came from a variety of places, some of which they shared with me: they had a student showing all the symptoms I had; they experienced it themselves, etc. If we can grasp the warning signs, we can, together, put an end to all of this.

One of the schools I spoke at was the same middle school that I attended whilst the entire Ted bullying was happening. In this school I was met with the widest range of reactions. Some cried with me as I cried explaining how exhausting it was to come to school every day hoping that Ted wouldn't be as harsh today.

I had teachers looking at me with no specific emotion, just watching and absorbing everything I had to say. There were also teachers who looked at me like they didn't quite believe what I was saying to them. This I understood in some way because I don't think I would have believed it if I was in their position and missed all the warning signs as well. I was even met with one look from a teacher I will never forget.

The teacher who I once had thought of as another mom looked at me with disdain. She stared into my eyes for the first half of the presentation looking so concerned, until I got to the part about her class. *Note: I never specified any names in any of these presentations.* After I started talking about how disappointed and hurt I was that not even she noticed or took action upon the matter, her eyes changed. She crossed her legs, turned her body away, and didn't look at me again for the rest of the time I was there.

At another school I had to present to another familiar face. Do you remember the teacher who teased me and by doing so condoned it for the rest of the class? Bingo. She had moved to another school and I was presenting there. Once she saw that I was presenting, she didn't look toward the front again. She never said a word to me afterward when other teachers and faculty came up to me to ask questions about the presentation. I didn't need an apology, but I did want to ask her why. Unfortunately, just like with Ted, I will never know why and that is something I will just have to learn to deal with.

The last middle school that came with a surprise for me was not a teacher I ever had but the mother of the girl who told me it was her happiest memory to see the agony I was put through. The mother, however, seemed to not show any sort of recognition that that girl could be her daughter. It just goes to show that you never know how much you really do know a person. She was one of the most concerned people at that school, and she would never know her daughter played a role in all of it.

All the schools I presented to shared similar reactions, and each of them had unique ones as well. In multiple schools I was given the chance to actually meet another person, usually a teacher, who had been just like me growing up: bullied and suicidal but has overcome it and grown from the experience in order to help stop it from happening to another. Some days I wish I had gone to one of these teachers because I know then it would have turned out differently.

Most days I recognize that I went through this for a reason. I, at the mere age of seventeen, am able to tell my story and become an advocate for all the lost souls out there begging for help but not getting it, begging to be seen but staying invisible, and wishing that the day comes where life has that haven we are all waiting for.

Not only do the teachers and parents need to be able to recognize these warnings signs but the young adults they are teaching do as well. Your friends are whom you rely on for some of the most significant things in life when you are at this age. If my friends had been able to see the warning signs of depression and being suicidal, they could have done something in order to help me deal with everything I was being put through. Looking back, I wonder whether my friends chose to ignore it, were too caught up in their own lives, or just didn't realize the significance of my behavior.

In order to make this book as well-rounded as possible I have gone to some of the friends whom I attended middle school with and asked questions about the bullying problems. Some of them never realized anyone would ever have picked on me because I was always the one to stop it for other kids. Other people didn't realize the Ted problem was bad enough to do anything about it because they figured I complained about the normal teenage things more than I ever complained about him. So his impact on me really was not noteworthy to them until after finding out the whole story years later. One of my close friends even said he had realized Ted did those things but never really pinpointed who Ted was always aiming it at.

One friend in particular was so upset when I told him about having been bullied. He wanted to know the name of the boy, and you could tell he wanted some type of action taken on my behalf. I then went on to explain that the action is being taken against Ted every day that I get up with a smile on my face thankful to be alive. In every word I type an action is being taken against him and everything he stood for. The action I am taking is the most powerful action that could ever be taken against it. I am overcoming having been through it and have my mind set to erase bullying from our world as much as humanly possible.

The friend took this answer but was still dumbfounded that anyone would have picked on me, of all people. What we get into here is that bully isn't always just a bully, and a victim doesn't always show the characteristics of someone whom you would expect to be bullied. I may have been nerdy, but I wasn't the girl that would rather sit in from lunch and do math equations than go outside. I wasn't the kid with the accent. I wasn't the girl whom everyone hated either. I was me. I did what I could to fit in when I needed to while always being true to myself. I refused to let people change me because they believed something else was right. I tried to always be there for anyone who needed me, whether I knew you since you were three or for three minutes.

SOME PAINS DON'T GO AWAY

Some days I still wake up to all the pain Ted caused me. I feel it wash over me like a tidal wave trying to pull me down into the sea of depression, and each day I find the strength to walk out of the tidal wave, and being able to do so allows me to see that Ted no longer has the same power over me as he once had. I may always feel anxiety at the thought of being near him, but that is to be expected with any kind of traumatic event.

RELIVING THE PAST

Whenever I find old homework assignments in my room or my parents' room I always flash back and see the Ted memories attached to them even after all these years. I broke down recently because I found the assignment on the Greek gods that Ted and I had made the agreement on. I was supposed to mention his character and he would stop bullying me. As I told you, before he obviously didn't. I cried hysterically after finding this. I saw his face laughing at me and telling me I don't belong and I'm nothing to the world. He tore me down three years later without even knowing it.

I wonder if he will ever stop being a part of my life. When will I really and truly be free from that part of my life? I hate knowing he still has a power over me. The words still sting. The actions are burned into my memory forever, but should I let it continue to break me down? Am I meant to end up with suicide as my last act? I question this every day, and every day I put a smile on my face and push to get through it. One day this smile will come easily, and one day I will recognize that Ted, in a way, blessed me.

....

BLESSING OR CURSE?

I have let it become a curse, but one day it will be a blessing. The day I stop and look back and see him as handing me what will become my life's passion will be the day I realize it is a blessing.

Lucky me, that day is today. I no longer need to shrink back from my tormentor. I was put through all this pain in order to stop it from ever happening to anyone else. People have been bullied since the beginning of time. People have had enormous difficulty coming to terms with their bullies and coming to terms with the reasons they were chosen to be bullied. I was chosen in order to speak out about all this pain that is locked away in every soul who has ever been bullied or harassed in any form.

We need an advocate for bullying to end. We need a plan to stop it. Talking in the schools is just step one. This book is step two. The rest of the steps will come into place as I continue my life's journey of ridding the world of this disease. Seeing it stopped will be a miracle. It is a miracle that I am still alive today. It is a miracle that I am able to speak out at such a young age. I am proof that miracles do happen. My plan is to stop bullying everywhere, starting in our schools where our children need to be safe because this is where guardians aren't there to protect them. My goal is massive, but my passion for it is even bigger.

Bullies are the same as victims in that there is no cookie-cutter person. People bully for different reasons.

They may have been bullied in grade school and finally wanted some sort of revenge on the matter.

They may have low self-esteem and raised theirs by lowering yours.

They could be a victim in their own household and need to take it out on someone away from their place of hurt.

They could see a familiar lack of self-worth in you that they feel everyday of their life.

We never know what can cause someone to become a bully. No matter the circumstance, though, it is never okay to purposely hurt any other person. We have to get to the heart of the problem, but in order to get to that we must get to the victims that we can see are being bullied, harassed, tormented, or even just teased.

SOMETHING BIGGER

My purpose in life is to make the significance of bullying known and recognized for what it truly is. I will continue to do whatever I can in order to help overcome the epidemic that is bullying. I only ask that you come with me in this fight against it. Together, we can completely wipe it from our schools and, eventually, our lives. I believe that with your support that we can truly accomplish the impossible and improbable. To me it is possible, and I know to you out there seeing your son, daughter, neighbor, or self in me believe it is possible too. I am able to do something that not every victim of bullying or person who has thought about suicide can; I can speak out about it in order to make ending it more than a possibility. I will make it into a reality.

Bullying is everywhere; it happens to everyone. Bullying has changed people's lives and ended people's lives.

Bullying has led us to this:

My name is Brandy Dolen, and I have Post-traumatic stress disorder as a result of being bullied in school.

15114852R10061

Made in the USA
Charleston, SC
18 October 2012